World's
Weirdest
Gadgets

Look for other

titles:
World's Weirdest Critters
Creepy Stuff
Odd-inary People
Amazing Escapes
Bizarre Bugs

World's Weirdest Gadgets

by Mary Packard

and the Editors of Ripley Entertainment Inc.

illustrations by Leanne Franson

SCHOLASTIC INC.

New York   Toronto   London   Auckland   Sydney
Mexico City   New Delhi   Hong Kong   Buenos Aires

Developed by Nancy Hall, Inc.
Designed by R studio T
Cover design by Atif Toor
Photo research by Laura Miller

ISBN 0-439-41767-8

12 11 10 9 8 7 6 5 4 3 2 1   2 3 4 5 6 7 / 0

Printed in the U.S.A.
First Scholastic printing, October 2002

Contents

Ripley's Believe It or Not!

World's Weirdest Gadgets

Introduction

The Man Who Reinvented Himself

Robert Ripley was one of the most unconventional personalities of the 20th century. He traveled the globe visiting amazing places, meeting incredible people, and gathering bizarre stories and artifacts to use in his Believe It or Not! cartoons. Although Ripley's subjects varied widely, they all had one underlying theme: The world is an unbelievably amazing place.

A self-taught artist, Ripley began his career earning $18 a week as a sports cartoonist. One day, when he couldn't think of a subject for the next day's cartoon, he put together a group of assorted athletic facts and feats from his personal files. Then he handed in his work and hoped for the best.

"The best" was far more spectacular than he could have imagined. This first Believe It or Not! cartoon was an overnight sensation. After Ripley expanded his column to include subjects from all areas of life, he became the first millionaire cartoonist in history. He wrote Believe It or Not! books, opened museums, starred

in a radio show, and soon after television was invented, had his own TV show.

Ripley's favorite subjects were those that celebrated the uniqueness of the human spirit. He particularly admired the kind of creativity and persistence it takes to become an inventor. He was fascinated by people who found completely fresh ways to view the occurrences of daily life—people like Sir Isaac Newton, who, after being hit on the head by an apple, figured out the principle of gravity. Or Archimedes, the Ancient Greek philosopher who noticed that when he lowered himself into the tub, the water level rose, prompting him to come up with a method to measure the volume of objects by seeing how much water they displaced.

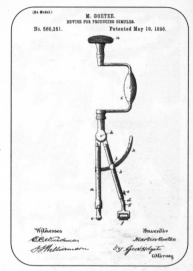

Robert Ripley also took great pleasure in showcasing funny inventions like dimple-makers, dogmobiles, and alarm clocks that sprayed water in a sleeper's face. Marvels of ingenuity like the mustache protector might have been forgotten if Ripley had not recorded them in his cartoons. And Ripley was especially impressed by the creations of inventors under 12 years old.

So get ready! You're about to discover a world of incredible inventions created by people just like you. Who knows? Maybe you'll be inspired to invent something totally incredible.

Believe It!®

Occasionally, things turn out even better than we expect.

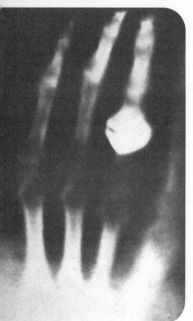

A Bright Idea: In 1895, German scientist Wilhelm Roentgen turned on his cathode-ray machine. A sheet of paper coated with a barium chemical compound immediately started to glow. Imagine Roentgen's surprise when he put his hand between the apparatus and the paper— and saw the outline of his bones. He later took the first X-ray photograph of his wife's left hand. In 1901, Roentgen was awarded the first Nobel Prize in physics for his discovery.

Imagine That!

In ancient China, the penalty for revealing the secret of making silk to foreigners was . . .

a. going naked.
b. death.
c. eating silkworms.
d. cutting out the tongue.

A Sticky Problem: While Spence Silver, a scientist at 3M Laboratories, was trying to come up with a superstrong glue in 1968, he came up with an adhesive that stuck, but only sort of. For years, Silver showed it to coworkers, hoping someone would figure out what to do with it. At last, Arthur Fry in new-product development thought of Silver's glue when his paper bookmarks kept falling out of his hymnal at choir practice. After Fry coated the bookmarks with the glue, they not only stayed in place, but could be removed without damaging the pages. The resulting product, Post-it Notes, is now among 3M's best-selling products.

W. Hunt.
Pin.
N° 6281.   Patented Apr. 10. 1849

Fig. 1.   Fig. 2.

Fig. 4.   Fig. 3.

Fig. 5.   Fig. 6.

Fig. 8   Fig. 7.

Wired: In 1849, Walter Hunt, an inventor who lived in New York City, was idly twisting a wire while trying to think of a way to earn enough money to pay off a $15 debt. The result was the safety pin. Hunt patented his invention, but had no idea of its potential value. He sold the rights for just $400.

Potluck: In the 1890s, Conrad Hubert bought the patent rights to a novelty item called the electric flowerpot. Out of the flowerpot "grew" a stem, which was actually a narrow tube containing a battery. A bulb lit up an artificial plant at its top. Unfortunately, there weren't many buyers. So Hubert decided to separate the tube and the lightbulb from the flowerpot and patent his new product as the Portable Electric Light. This early flashlight was an instant success, and Hubert formed the American Ever-Ready Company and made his fortune.

Imagine That!

According to the U.S. Patent and Trademark Office, an invention is sometimes the product of . . .

a. absolute genius.
b. sheer stupidity.
c. smoke and mirrors.
d. pure luck.

Explosive Discovery:

In 1826, an English pharmacist named John Walker was trying to invent a new explosive. After stirring up a batch of chemicals, he set the mixture aside. Later, he saw that a glob had hardened at the end of his stirring stick, and he tried to get it off by scraping the stick against the floor. Much to his surprise, the glob burst into flames. Walker had accidentally invented the first friction match.

All Fired Up: When untreated, rubber, which is made from tree sap, melts in hot weather and cracks in the cold. During the winter of 1839, British scientist Charles Goodyear was experimenting with ways to make it better. While heating rubber mixed with sulfur, he and his brother began to argue. As Goodyear gestured wildly with his stirrer, he dropped some of the goop onto the hot stove. Later, he scraped the rubber off and was amazed to find that it was dry and flexible. He put some outside, and in the morning, found that the rubber had not cracked in the cold. Goodyear's process is called *vulcanization*.

Imagine That!

Microwaves produce heat by . . .

a. causing molecules in food to rub against each other.
b. creating tiny waves of gas.
c. producing electromagnetic fields.
d. creating thermodynamic fumes.

Marvelous Meltdown: The magnetron tube, which produces microwave radiation, was first used in radar sets during World War II. In 1946, while testing one of the tubes at Raytheon Laboratories, a scientist named Percy Spencer reached into his pocket for a candy bar and found a warm, gooey mess. Aware that microwaves produced heat, Spencer wondered if the melting was caused by the magnetron. To test his theory, he put a bag of popcorn kernels next to the magnetron. Before he knew it, the kernels were popping all over the floor. Spencer had his answer—and the key to microwave cooking!

Shoe-In: Patsy Sherman, a researcher at 3M Laboratories, was working with fluorochemicals to be used in the airplane industry. In 1953, a lab assistant spilled a bit of an experimental mixture onto her new sneakers. The assistant tried to clean it off, but neither soap nor solvents worked. As time went on, the area inside the chemical spill stayed white, while the rest of the shoe got dirty. Sherman took notice and along with Sam Smith, another 3M chemist, set out to improve the new fabric protector. The product, launched in 1956, was spectacularly successful. Its name? Scotchgard.

Dry Idea: One day, Jean-Baptiste Jolly, a French tailor, knocked over an oil lamp and spilled turpentine on a tablecloth. As he tried to clean up the mess, he noticed that the more he rubbed, the brighter the fabric became. Jolly recognized the value of his discovery at once. He called his new cleaning method *dry cleaning*, and in 1825 opened the world's first dry-cleaning store in Paris.

Child's Play: While working at his father's company in Ohio, Joe McVicker came up with a new cleaning product, but it was so weird and pasty he wasn't sure what to do with it. On a hunch, he wiped it over some smudges on the wallpaper in his office, and they disappeared. But even though his Magic Wallpaper Cleaner worked well, it didn't sell. After McVicker's sister-in-law told him that the children at her nursery school found clay hard to work with because their hands were so small, he sent samples of his nontoxic cleaner for the kids to play with. This time his hunch paid off. The kids had a ball with it. By 1957, color and fragrance had been added, and the name of the former wallpaper cleaner was changed to one we all know: Play-Doh.

Imagine That!

The fragrance that was added to Play-Doh is . . .

a. cinnamon.
b. mint.
c. ginger.
d. vanilla.

Good Vibrations: In 1945, engineer Richard James was trying to produce a spring that would keep the needles on ship gauges from bouncing around with the motion of the waves. One day, he accidentally knocked his model off a shelf. The spring moved coil by coil from the shelf to a table to a chair, only to land upright on the floor. Next, he tried it on the stairs. When his wife saw it, she instantly realized what a wonderful toy it would make. She named it Slinky and started the company that has continued producing the creation to this very day.

Presidential Bearing: In 1902, the *Washington Star* published a cartoon featuring President Theodore "Teddy" Roosevelt, rifle in hand, walking away from a frightened bear cub. It was based on a real-life incident. During a hunting trip, Roosevelt's hosts wanted to ensure he got a trophy, so they trapped a cub for him to shoot. Roosevelt refused. Morris Michtom displayed the cartoon clipping in his shop window next to a stuffed bear cub made by his wife. To his surprise, everyone wanted to buy "Teddy's Bear." To meet the demand, Michtom started his own manufacturing company, later known as the Ideal Toy Corporation.

Not So Silly: What stretches, bounces, shatters when hit with a hammer, and picks up lint from clothing, and print from newspapers and comic books? In 1943, General Electric engineer James Wright was trying to create an inexpensive rubber substitute. In one experiment, Wright added boric acid to silicon oil. What he got was a slippery substance that bounced. What could you do with it? Nothing practical, Wright thought. Maybe not, but in 1950, Peter Hodgson bought $147 worth of the gooey stuff, put it inside plastic eggs, and sold it as a toy called Silly Putty. Since then, more than three hundred million of the toy have been sold.

Imagine That!

Which of the following statements is not true about Silly Putty?

a. Athletes use it to strengthen hand muscles.
b. Zookeepers have used it to create paw imprints of gorillas.
c. Orthodontists use it to create dental molds.
d. Astronauts used it to anchor objects on Apollo 8.

Chipped Off: George Crum was the chef at an elegant restaurant in Saratoga Springs, New York. One day in 1853, a very demanding customer kept sending back his French fries because they weren't thin enough. The third time they came back, Crum sliced the potatoes paper-thin, then purposely fried them to a crisp. Much to Crum's surprise, the customer was delighted, and so was everyone else who sampled them. Word of the taste sensation spread throughout the area, and people traveled great distances to sample the new Saratoga Chips. After the automatic potato slicer was invented in the 1920s, potato chips became America's best-selling snack food.

Imagine That!

To make enough potato chips each year to satisfy the craving of United States consumers, you would need more than . . .

a. 100,000 pounds of potatoes.
b. three billion pounds of potatoes.
c. 500,000 tons of potatoes.
d. 10 million bushels of potatoes.

Cold Comfort: In 1875, a law was passed in Evanston, Illinois, banning the sale of ice-cream sodas on Sunday. Carbonated beverages were thought to be related to alcoholic beverages and, as such, could not be sold on a day of worship. Undaunted, shop owners simply removed the soda

and served the scoops of ice cream with syrup. They called the new treats *sundaes* to distinguish them from the spelling of the Christian Sabbath day.

Play with Your Food: The sandwich was named after the Earl of Sandwich, who loved to gamble. He invented it so he could eat a meal without interrupting his card game.

Dye-ing of Thirst: Pete Conklin invented pink lemonade in the 1800s when he unwittingly made lemonade from a bucket of water in which a circus performer had soaked his red tights.

Hole-in-One: One night in the 1800s, a storm came up while Captain Hanson Gregory was at sea. He anchored the fried cake he'd been eating on one of the spokes of the helm so that he could use both hands to steer. When he retrieved his cake, Gregory was pleased to note that the part he liked least—the soggy middle—was gone. From then on, he had the cook fry his cakes with a hole in the center. A less exciting story has Gregory's mother complaining that the centers of her cakes didn't cook through, and the young Gregory suggesting that she try making them with a hole in the middle. In either event, Gregory gets the credit for inventing the doughnut as we know it.

Half-Baked: In 1930, Ruth Wakefield, owner and proprietor of the Toll House Inn in Massachusetts, was baking chocolate cookies when she realized that she was out of baker's chocolate. So she broke up  some of the semisweet chocolate she had on hand and stirred the pieces into the dough. When she removed the cookies from the oven, Wakefield saw that the chocolate had not dissolved. She served the chocolate chip cookies anyway and was amazed at the delighted response of her customers. Chocolate chip cookies have since become an American favorite.

Fill 'er Up: Italo Marchiony of New York was granted a patent for an ice-cream cone in 1903. But several others claim it was invented at the 1904 World's Fair in St. Louis, Missouri. In one story, Ernest Hamwi was selling wafflelike pastries next to an ice-cream vendor who ran out of dishes. Hamwi rolled a pastry into a cone shape, and the ice-cream vendor filled it with a scoop of ice cream. They called it the World's Fair Cornucopia.

Windfall: In 2737 B.C.E., Chinese emperor Shen Nong was outside boiling water when falling leaves accidentally landed in his kettle. As the leaves began to brew, the aroma was so enticing that the emperor took a taste. The flavor was both soothing and refreshing—and people have been drinking tea ever since.

Ripley's Believe It or Not! **Brain Buster**

Your turn! Bust your brain on these "inventive" activities. Some creations made history—others are just made up. Can you tell the difference?

Robert Ripley dedicated his life to seeking out the bizarre and unusual. But every unbelievable thing he recorded was true. In the Brain Busters at the end of each chapter, you'll play Ripley's role—trying to verify the fantastic facts presented. Each Ripley's Brain Buster contains a group of four shocking statements. But of these so-called "facts," **one** is **fiction**. Will you **Believe It!** or **Not!**?

Wait—there's more! Following the Brain Busters are special bonus games where you can try to keep those Ripley's facts straight by playing matchup. To see how you did, flip to the end of the book for answer keys and a scorecard.

How *did* you think of that?!! Well, people come up with inventions in all sorts of ways. Here are four wacky innovation stories. Can you tell which three are true and which one is pure invention?

a. The Frisbee was modeled after pie tins that students at Yale University would throw around for fun in the 1870s. The tins came from a local pie maker named (what else?) William Frisbie.

Believe It!   **Not!**

19

b. Amanda Jones is the woman responsible for the vacuum method of canning that revolutionized the food industry. But Jones claimed that the idea was not hers at all—she insisted that her dead brother came to her in a vision and told her to try it.

Believe It!   Not!

c. Early versions of the Hula Hoop were made out of vines and wood quite some time ago. Records of their existence date back to ancient Egypt and Greece.

Believe It!   Not!

d. Steven R. Goodman, inventor of the sidewalk, claims the idea came to him after he sat on his head for five hours straight, staring at a freshly paved road.

Believe It!   Not!

• •

BONUS GAME

Name Game! **Many inventions improved upon items that already existed. And most have changed names over the course of time. The following are five common items. Can you match them up to the names they once had?**

1. Kool-Aid
2. Life Savers
3. Bubble gum
4. Vacuum cleaner
5. Zipper

a. Blibber-Blubber
b. Pneumatic carpet renovator
c. Fruit Smack
d. Pep-O-Mint
e. Clasp-locker

It's not too hard to figure out why some inventions do *not* stand the test of time.

Fish in a Barrel: In the 1800s, Jules Le Batteux of France believed that hands-on experience was the best kind. Perhaps that's why he invented a new way to fish. Lowering himself into the water in a barrel fitted with a leather sleeve and glove, Batteux put his hand into the glove and grabbed the fish as they swam by.

Imagine That!

An alarm clock invented in 1500 sounded the hour and also . . .

a. ran a bath.
b. let out the dog.
c. watered the plants.
d. lit a candle.

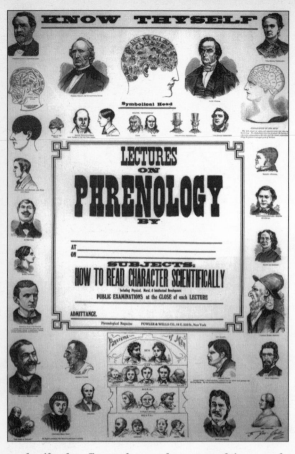

Getting Your Head Examined: Phrenology is the study of personality and character traits based on the shape of a person's skull. Phrenologists figured that the skull took its shape from the brain, and you could "read" a person's skull like a map. In 1901, Henry C. Lavery of Wisconsin built the first phrenology machine and called it the psychograph. While the subject sat in a chair beneath a headpiece, the machine measured 32 mental faculties and rated them from "deficient" to "very superior." The data was sent to a printer that produced readings on paper tape. Once considered a foolproof way to make important life decisions—such as whom to marry or what career to choose—today, psychographs are found only in places like the Ripley's Odditoriums and the Museum of Questionable Medical Devices.

Diet Fork: If you tend to gulp your food, a fork with a built-in timer might be the perfect thing for you. This fork tells its owner when it's okay to take another bite. By the time you're halfway through, the odds are your food will be so cold you won't even want it anymore.

Grapefruit Guard: You won't get a spray in the eye from your grapefruit if you wear a grapefruit mask at breakfast.

Imagine That!

At the age of 82, Edgar Sims of Sun City, Arizona, invented a hearing aid in the shape of . . .

a. mouse ears.
b. a conch shell.
c. a megaphone.
d. antennae.

Bottoms Up: For those beginning skiers who spend a lot of time on their butts, the Laid-Back Skiers Association invented special skis to be worn—where else?—on the rear end!

Dull Idea: Herbert Greene of Pennsylvania invented a knife with a slot in the blade that would keep those pesky peas from rolling off your knife while eating.

Crying Time:

Patented in 1971, an electrical device designed to put a baby to sleep with a series of regular pats on the bottom seemed to make the baby cry even harder.

Whiff-le Ball:

A golf ball that glows and gives off a scent so it can be easily found was invented and patented in 1990.

Sleeping Beauties:

Why bury the dead when you can keep your loved one preserved and hermetically sealed in a decorative block of glass? This invention, which received U.S. patent #748,284 in 1903, would also make a nifty coffee table.

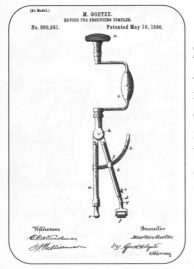

Smile!

A device for making dimples was invented by Martin Goetze in 1896.

Imagine That!

Over 300 patents have been registered with the U.S. Patent Office for devices to stop . . .

a. fingernail-biting.
b. snoring.
c. bed-wetting.
d. stuttering.

Stiff Upper Lip: In 1872, Eli J. F. Randolph of New York invented a mustache protector. A hard rubber device with prongs that fit into the nostrils, it was designed to keep mustaches neat and tidy while eating and drinking. To date, it has not found its market.

Don't Forget to Dunk Your Watch: A watch powered by water, milk, tea, or any other type of liquid must be dunked every few days to keep it running on time.

Following Suits: Invented by Mark Woehrer of Nebraska, Tag-a-long, the robotic suitcase carrier that follows its owner wherever he or she goes, has yet to catch on.

What a Scream! For all those stressed-out souls who need a harmless outlet, the scream muffler is just what the doctor ordered. All they have to do is scream at the top of their lungs into the scream muffler. No one will hear them because it is packed with special acoustical foam that will turn even the loudest screech into the softest whimper.

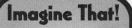
Edison's Follies: Thomas A. Edison was granted 1,093 U.S. patents. Many of his revolutionary inventions

changed our lives forever, but not all of them were winners. Take, for instance, his concrete houses, which were supposed to be cheap and easy to build. Unfortunately, before even one house could go up, a builder had to buy almost $200,000 worth of equipment—and the iron forms required to hold the poured concrete weighed nearly half a million pounds!

Guess What Time It Is: The one-hand clock invented by Benjamin Franklin in 1770 gave you a choice. For example, the time could be 3:35, 7:35, or 11:35. Franklin figured that everyone knew what hour of the day it was. A 1919 version (at right) took away the guessing by setting up the hours as on a normal clock, but showing all 60 minutes for each hour.

Kitchen Helper: A device that served as a combination grater, slicer, mouse trap, and fly trap was given U.S. patent #586,025 in 1897.

Plow and Shoot: In 1862, a patent on an invention that worked as a combined plow and gun was filed at the U.S. Patent Office.

Tip-Off:

Just the thing for a cold winter stroll, U.S. patent #556,248 is for an invention that makes it possible for a gentleman to tip his hat while keeping his hands in his pockets.

How Convenient!

A topcoat patented in 1953 by Howard Ross of Gainesville, Virginia, could be worn by one person or expanded to fit two.

Imagine That!

A patent was filed at the U.S. Patent Office for a bicycle security device. If it wasn't disarmed by its owner, it would send up through the bicycle seat . . .

a. a needle.
b. superglue.
c. an electric shock.
d. an icy spray of water.

Suited to Your Mood: Because it is thermally sensitive, a bathing suit invented by Donald Spector of Union City, New Jersey, changes color as its wearer's body temperature fluctuates according to his or her mood.

Over the Top: In 1895, Henry Latimer Simmons of Wickes, Montana, patented a railroad system featuring cars that had tracks on their sloped roofs. This made it possible for one train to leapfrog over another while traveling on a single track.

Spare the Child: A spanking paddle, patented in the U.S. in 1953, had a jointed handle designed to break if the child was spanked too firmly.

Wet Blanket: In 1907, an alarm clock that sprayed water on a sleeping person received U.S. patent #889,928.

Imagine That!

Rick Tweddell of Ohio invented plastic molds that change the shape of growing vegetables to make them look like . . .

a. dogs and cats.
b. famous people.
c. letters of the alphabet.
d. different kinds of cars.

Pucker Up:

In the 1930s, Hollywood makeup artist Max Factor invented a hand-operated kissing machine with molded rubber lips that could be pressed together to test lipstick.

Double Play:

James Bennett invented a double baseball glove in 1905. The player wore one part in each hand and caught the ball by clapping his or her hands together.

Rude Awakening:

Have trouble rising and shining? Perhaps you need a contraption invented by Ludwig Ederer of Omaha, Nebraska, to automatically throw you out of bed. Connected to steam pipes, the bed would lower and dump the sleeper when the pressure fell.

Dying to Escape:

Being buried alive was of grave concern to those living in the late 1800s and early 1900s. Luckily for them, Count Karnice-Karnicki of Russia invented a solution in 1896. A glass ball was connected by a spring to a box above the grave. If the chest of

the buried person moved, the spring was released and the box lid popped open, letting light and air reach the coffin. It also rang a bell and raised a flag to alert unsuspecting mourners.

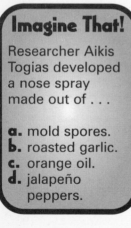

Imagine That!

Researcher Aikis Togias developed a nose spray made out of . . .

a. mold spores.
b. roasted garlic.
c. orange oil.
d. jalapeño peppers.

Heads Up:

In 1962, George R. Masters invented a device for a player to practice passing a football to him- or herself. It consisted of a headband with a football attached by an elastic cord.

But Why?

Thomas Urquhart, a 17th-century English translator, invented a language that consisted entirely of palindromes—words that can be read forward or backward.

Safety Briefs: In 1998, Katsuo Katugoru of Tokyo, Japan, whose greatest fear is drowning, designed underpants that would inflate 30 times their original size if there were a tidal wave. Unfortunately, Katugoru accidentally set them off while riding on a crowded subway at rush hour. Fortunately, one passenger had the presence of mind to deflate the underpants by stabbing them with a pencil.

Eyesore: Invented in 1931, the eyeball massager was operated by squeezing its two rubber centers.

Putting a Lid on It: Inventor of the alternating current motor and many other successful inventions, Nikola Tesla tried but was unsuccessful in perfecting a device that could photograph thoughts on the eyeball.

Fish Story: For better night fishing, Canadian Paul Giannaris invented a chemical formula that makes worms glow in the dark.

Scaredy-Cat: Uninvited creatures are supposed to scurry from your garden when they see the amazing mechanical leaping cat, which is guaranteed to keep your garden pest-free.

Imagine That!

The Ohio Department of Transportation is studying ways to use fermented cheese as a . . .

a. warning flare.
b. paving material.
c. dye for highway stripes.
d. deicer on highways.

Kooky contraptions! Though the following discoveries may have missed the history books, three of the stories are true. One, however, is nothing but a tall tale.

a. With his head in the sky, William Calderwood of Sun City, Arizona, dreamed of floating furniture. He crafted it so that it could stay in the air for up to six weeks.
Believe It!   Not!

b. Singing and stitching must have been in fashion when, in the 1800s, a sewing machine was invented that also played music.
Believe It!   Not!

c. In 1974, a picture frame equipped with voice recording technology was invented in Hobart, Indiana, by D. Butler. The device allowed people to gaze at photographs while listening to a recorded message up to two and one-half minutes in length.
Believe It!   Not!

d. In 1887, Charles Wulff patented a bird-powered balloon propelled by eagles, vultures, and condors.
Believe It!   Not!

BONUS GAME

Who needs it? Some inventions seem utterly useless, while others make us wonder how we ever lived without them. But in fact there was a time before our everyday items existed. Can you place these familiar objects in the order in which they made their much-needed debuts?

1. Envelopes

2. Postcards

3. Jigsaw puzzles

4. Common cross-blade scissors

5. Basketball hoops

a. 3 (1839)

b. 4 (1869)

c. 1 (1500)

d. 5 (1906)

e. 2 (1760)

CHAPTER 3 Way to Go!

There's no limit to the lengths, heights, and depths people will go to when looking for new ways to get around.

Having It Your Way:

AUTOnomy, General Motors' new concept car, is controlled by wires and software, and powered by hydrogen fuel cells, which won't give off harmful emissions such as carbon dioxide. And for the style-conscious, the car would be manufactured in two parts—the chassis, called a "skateboard," and the body—so you could buy a short, medium, or long chassis to match whichever style body you prefer.

Imagine That!

In 1900, Uriah Smith of Battle Creek, Michigan, designed a horseless carriage that, in order not to frighten horses, featured . . .

a. simulated hoofbeats.
b. no bright colors or shiny metal.
c. a model of a horse's head in front.
d. a whisper-quiet motor.

Lunar Buggy:
Using nothing more high-tech than scrap aluminum, an old umbrella, bicycle handlebars, automobile hubcaps, a starter motor, batteries, and army surplus stock,

Eduardo Carrion San Juan of San Jose, California, designed and invented the prototype of the lunar roving vehicle used to explore the moon.

Front-Wheel Drive: A dogmobile, patented in the United States in 1870, was propelled by two dogs running in a cage inside the front wheels.

Details, Details: A flying automobile was successfully flown in the United States in 1947, but crashed because the pilot had forgotten to fill the gas tank.

Slow and Steady:

Invented by David Bushnell of Saybrook, Connecticut, the *Turtle* was the first submarine ever to be used in a war. About seven feet high and seven feet long, the wooden vessel

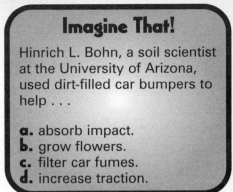

was bound by iron hoops and hand-powered by one person. On September 7, 1776, Ezra Lee set off in the *Turtle* to plant a bomb on a British ship in New York harbor. After failing to attach the device to the ship's hull, Lee released it in the harbor, where it blew up, reportedly startling the British fleet, which promptly sailed to safer waters.

Look Out, Bell-ow!

A diving bell, enabling divers to work at the bottom of the sea for hours, was invented in 1720 by English astronomer Edmund Halley, who also predicted the cycle of the comet that became known as Halley's Comet.

Making a Splash:

A diving suit invented by Hardsuits International is an atmospheric diving system that stabilizes air pressure around the body so that divers can work comfortably at depths of 2,000 feet. The suit is powered by twin motors on either side of the oxygen tank, and divers can steer in any direction by using the built-in foot pedals. Because the suit weighs 1,100 pounds, divers have to be lowered into the water in a metal cage. Intending to use them for salvage and rescue missions, the U.S. Navy purchased four suits in 2001—at a cost of 2.7 million dollars each.

Imagine That!

A device for lifting vessels over sandbars was patented on May 22, 1849, by . . .

a. Robert Fulton.
b. Thomas A. Edison.
c. Benjamin Franklin.
d. Abraham Lincoln.

Making Waves:

Flat surf? No problem. The PowerSki Jetboard, invented by former surfer Bob Montgomery, makes its own waves. Combining the ease of waterskiing with the freedom of surfing, the Jetboard has a small but powerful engine that weighs just under 40  pounds. As of June 2002, you could get one for just under six thousand dollars.

Sub Cycle: In 1896, Alvary Templo of New York built the first underwater bicycle. A submarine-shaped air tank piped air to Templo's helmet, enabling him to stay down for as long as six hours.

Flying Solo: Imagine a flying machine that is almost as compact and easy to operate as a bicycle. Impossible? Not if Michael Moshier, founder of Millennium Jet in California, has his way. His SoloTrek XFV (short for Exoskeletor Flying Vehicle) supports two gas engine-powered fans that extend above the frame like giant ears. The pilot stands on a pair of footrests, tightens the body belt, and grabs onto the joysticks that control the vehicle. To date, the SoloTrek has only flown about eight inches off the ground for about nine seconds. But with support from the Pentagon and NASA, chances are that one day Moshier's dream machine will soar 8,000 feet above the trees at 80 miles per hour, just as it was designed to do.

Sky-Driving: California-based Paul Moller is perfecting his two-passenger M400 Skycar, which will fly like an airplane but can take off vertically like a helicopter.

Fire-Breather: Used by the Chinese in 11th-century warfare, the Fire Dragon was the world's first steam-driven land vehicle and also the world's first two-stage rocket. On its way to the target, the rocket ignited arrows that flew from the Dragon's mouth.

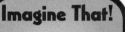

Rockets for Rookies:

Jeff Greason of Mojave, California, has invented the first reusable rocket engine. Greason's EZ-Rocket (above) is powered by twin 400-pound thrust rocket engines that burn isopropyl alcohol and liquid oxygen. The invention is capable of rising 65 miles into the air—high enough for a spectacular view, but not high enough to go into orbit. Greason estimates that someday such a tour could cost just $900 per flight, a real bargain when it comes to space travel.

Imagine That!

Before entering the automobile industry, David Buick invented the . . .

a. pushpin.
b. pacemaker.
c. porcelainized bathtub.
d. pulley.

Treading Water:

In July 1883, it took Jack Ferry eight hours to cross the English Channel on the giant tricycle he invented. Its extra-large rubber tires kept him afloat.

Roll Model: Two San Francisco designers, Johan Liden and Yves Behar, have come up with a prototype for Scoot, a sleek high-tech scooter. Made of carbon fiber and aluminum, Scoot combines a wide, scooped-out footrest with tough oversized wheels. It folds in two and its wheels tuck neatly away so that it can be slung over the shoulder when not in use. Powered by hydrogen, Scoot is made for speed, and once it becomes widely available, it's sure to leave its competitors far behind.

Imagine That!

In the late 1800s, an advertisement for the first bicycles described them as . . .

a. a well-balanced vehicle for a well-balanced traveler.
b. an ever-saddled horse that eats nothing.
c. a two-wheeled horseless cart.
d. a peddler's delight.

Miles to Go: Created by Italian bike-maker Aprilia, the first electric bike powered by pollution-free hydrogen gas is scheduled to be available in 2003. It weighs less than regular electric bikes and travels twice the distance—43 miles—before it needs more fuel.

Wheels of Fortune: Dean Kamen believes his gyroscope-stabilized, battery-powered scooter known as the Segway will replace the car in cities. A single battery charge will take Segway owners 15 miles over level ground. Speed and direction are controlled by the driver shifting his or her weight. Currently, the Segway is being tested by mail carriers in New Hampshire.

Plugged In: Steve Roberts of Washington traveled 17,000 miles on a high-tech, 580-pound bicycle called the BEHEMOTH. It featured 105 gears, five computers, satellite connection to the Internet, an amateur radio, and a handlebar keyboard that let him write while riding. Where was the computer display? In his helmet!

Roll Playing: Jean-Yves Blondeau has invented a new way to skate. In addition to standard in-line skates, he wears a bodysuit made of hard latex with wheels attached at the knees, back, elbows, hands, and chest— 27 in total. As he zips through the streets of Paris at speeds of up to 30 miles per hour, he can morph into 20 perfectly balanced positions. To excel at Blondeau's new sport, you need the agility of a hockey player and the balance and flexibility of a gymnast.

Big Wheels: An eight-man tricycle built in New England in 1896 weighed 2,500 pounds, was 17 feet long, and had rear wheels that were 11 feet in diameter.

Imagine That!

A trolley car designed in the 1870s had an engine that ran on . . .

a. ammonia.
b. hay.
c. hydrogen.
d. apple peelings.

Moving right along . . . some inventions have taken us quite far. But one of the following four is _far_ from true!

a. In an effort to liven up the slopes, Daniel Cook of Princeton, New Jersey, invented snow skis equipped with radios and multicolored lights. He is currently working on a similar model for water skis.

Believe It!   **Not!**

b. A 16-passenger vehicle was created in 1827 by George Pocock. It was propelled by two huge kites flying from a single cord.

Believe It!   **Not!**

c. The Amphibian Marsh Buggy was a combination of car, tractor, and boat. With 10-foot-tall wheels, the buggy was used to navigate the Florida Everglades.

Believe It!   **Not!**

d. Robert Edison Fulton Jr. designed an airplane that could be converted into a car by removing its wings, propeller, and tail.

Believe It!   **Not!**

BONUS GAME

Get up and go! And while you're at it, connect these five modes of transportation to their "birthplace."

1. Motorcycle   **a.** New Hampshire, USA
2. Submarine   **b.** France
3. Roller skate   **c.** Holland
4. Snowmobile   **d.** Cannstadt, Germany
5. Ambulance   **e.** The Netherlands

CHAPTER 4 It Works!

All inventions start out with an idea. Sometimes the idea results from pure serendipity—other times it's the result of finding a problem that needs solving.

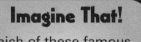

Fasten-ating Idea: Swiss scientist George de Mestral invented Velcro in the 1940s after studying burrs he found clinging to his clothing when he returned home from a walk through the fields.

Imagine That!

Which of these famous American inventors was kidnapped as a baby and ransomed for a horse?

a. Thomas Edison
b. George Washington Carver
c. Benjamin Franklin
d. Eli Whitney

The Right Touch: In 1829, Louis Braille, who was blind from birth, invented a way for the blind to read. He got the idea from French army troops, who punched marks in thick paper when sending messages so that they could "read" them in the dark trenches at night.

49

The *Real* Real McCoy: In the 1800s, inventor Elijah McCoy, the son of slaves, made a lubrication system that was so popular, buyers routinely inquired if they were getting "the real McCoy." To this day, when nothing else will do, people still insist on having "the real McCoy."

Crime Wave: In 1906, Lee De Forest invented a type of vacuum tube that greatly amplified weak radio signals. Unfortunately, before its true worth was realized, De Forest was arrested for selling stock in his invention, which was thought to be nothing but worthless glass.

Strong Suit: Having once survived an encounter with a grizzly bear, Troy Hurtubise invented a suit that is 50 times stronger and 85% lighter than steel so he could observe the big animals without putting himself in danger. To test it out, he stood in front of a brick wall while a car suspended on wires was swung into his chest like a pendulum. The 35,000-pound impact decimated the brick wall, yet left its wearer unharmed.

Keeping Current:

When his wife died in 1829, Samuel Morse was away from home at the time, and the news took a week to reach him. Grief-stricken, Morse, an artist, boarded a ship with the hope of finding some distraction in the art

galleries of Europe. On his return trip, he heard an American scientist lecture that "electric current is instantaneous." In college, Morse had learned that electricity is fluid. Perhaps, he reasoned, the current could be interrupted and clicks could be made by an electromagnet opening and closing the circuit—a short click for a dot and long one for a dash. If such a thing were possible, people would not have to wait weeks to get life-altering messages. Morse experimented with his idea for years and finally, in 1844, the first telegraph line was strung and the first message instantly communicated from Baltimore to Washington, D.C.

Imagine That!

In 1837, Thomas Davenport of Brandon, Vermont, patented America's first electric motor. He wound its magnet with silk from his . . .

a. top hat.
b. necktie.
c. wife's wedding dress.
d. own silkworms.

High-Tech Cattle Calls: In Japan, researchers have invented pagers for cows so that they can be beeped to come to the barn at milking time.

Just Spit It Out: Spitting out toothpaste could get very messy in a gravity-free environment, so a toothpaste that can be swallowed was invented especially for astronauts.

Painless Panes: You've heard of self-cleaning ovens. Now PPG Industries in Pittsburgh, Pennsylvania, has come up with a self-cleaning glass called SunClean. SunClean glass is lined with a transparent coating that breaks down dirt and bird droppings in the sun. When it rains, the remaining residue washes away without streaking.

Imagine That!

The first full-length movie ever shown on TV was called *The Heart of New York*. It was about the invention of . . .

a. the skyscraper.
b. the subway.
c. the washing machine.
d. neon lights.

Out of the Mouths of Wasps: René Antoine Ferchault de Réaumur was walking through the woods in the early days of the 18th century when he passed a wasp's nest. When he examined it, he saw that it was made from a crude form of paper. He concluded that the wasps had digested tiny bits of wood to produce the paper. Thus the idea for the modern process of making paper from wood was born.

On the Ball: A company in Illinois has developed a baseball that displays the speed at which it is thrown.

Can Do: In 1999, a research company in London, England, developed a "smart" garbage can that is able to read bar codes and sort waste into separate recycling bins. The can also records which items the household has run out of and needs to replace.

Mini-bots: Sometimes the only way to get inside tight spaces is to dismantle them. Soon it may be possible to send in the Mini Autonomous Robot Vehicle Jr. (MARV Jr. for short) to do the job. The size of a cherry and equipped

with tanklike treads, MARV Jr. could crawl through pipes or between walls. Its builders at Sandia National Laboratories hope to add a radio so MARV Jr. robots can communicate with humans—and with one another, so that they can work in swarms, like insects.

Slugging It Out: The SlugBot is a lawn mower-sized machine with a long arm that shines red light on the ground to identify slugs. When it finds one, it picks it up and drops it in a storage bin. When the bin is full, the SlugBot heads for a processor equipped with bacteria that will gobble up the slugs and convert them into a natural gas. The gas is then put into a fuel cell that in turn powers the SlugBot—so it can go out and collect more slugs.

Cool Idea:

Sometimes brilliance lies in simplicity, as a low-tech invention by Nigerian teacher Mohammed Bah Abba has proved. His rural area has no electricity, so there are no refrigerators. With no safe way to preserve leftover food, it had to be thrown away. Bah Abba's invention has changed that.

One earthenware pot is placed inside a larger one and the space between them is filled with moist sand. The inner pot is filled with vegetables and the whole thing is covered with a wet cloth. As water in the sand evaporates through the surface of the outer pot, the heat in the inner pot is drawn out and carried away. The vegetables can last for three weeks or more. Bah Abba gave away 12,000 of his Pot-in-Pot Preservation/Cooling Systems. Later, he sold them for 40 cents each to help cover the cost of manufacturing.

In 2000, Bah Abba received a $75,000 Rolex Award for Enterprise, which he plans to use to expand his distribution throughout northern Nigeria.

Imagine That!

The hourglass was invented in order to limit the length of . . .

a. sermons.
b. hard-boiling eggs.
c. doctors' house calls.
d. chess moves.

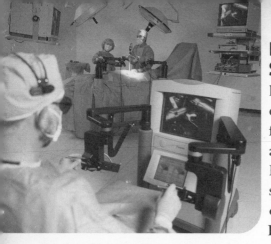

Remote-Control Surgery: Closed-chest heart surgery was developed by NASA for operating on astronauts in space. Here on Earth, surgeon Douglas Boyd operated on John Penner, a farmer who had suffered a heart attack but could not be away from his work for the three months he'd need to recover from conventional heart surgery. On October 6, 1999, in an operating room that looked like the site of a virtual-reality game, holes less than one-fourth of an inch wide were made in Penner's chest so three robotic arms could fit inside and perform the surgery. Dr. Boyd, sitting six feet away from his patient, guided the arms by remote control. The operation was a success, and the recovery period was so drastically reduced that Penner was back tending his cows in three days.

On the Beam:

A motorized wheelchair can be operated by eye movements, which interrupt a light beam when the user wears special glasses.

LOCO MOTION

Ever since the wheel was invented, people have continued the quest to find faster, cheaper, and more exciting ways to get around.

Balloonatic: In 2001, Ian Ashpole (see arrow) rose 11,000 feet in the air while attached to 600 ordinary party balloons. Here, he drifts alongside an enormous hot-air balloon advertising butter.

Roll, Roll, Roll Your Boat: Lyndon Yorke, inventor of a wicker car and the *Tritanic,* a tricycle catamaran (right), was named Best British Eccentric of 2001.

Cool Fuel: Bo Nordell, a researcher at Sweden's Luleå University of Technology, invented the Icy-Rider, a kind of go-cart, which can go 40 miles per hour—fueled only by freezing water!

What's That Again?

Rowland Emett's fanciful machines may not be very practical but they're sure to produce a smile and a giggle.

Hot Stuff: It may not breathe fire, but the Little Dragon Carpet Cleaner (left) wears eyeglasses with high-magnification lenses for optimum dirt-finding performance.

How Sweet It Is! Who wouldn't love to own the Humbug-Major Sweet Machine (below) to supply an endless amount of caramel apples and candy on demand?

Easy Rocker: A silent hot-air engine rocks the Hush-a-Bye Hot-Air Rocking Chair (above) by pushing a wheel back and forth on the floor.

Necessity was definitely not the mother of these inventions!

Little Shots: Master miniaturist Harry Libowitz of Brooklyn, New York, built a functional miniature pool table. He also built the world's smallest cameras. They stand 5.75 inches high on collapsible tripods, and can actually take pictures.

Itsy Bitsy Tea Set: A gold tea set that fits inside a gold locket is one tiny treasure from the Jules Charbneau collection. Inside the lid is Charbneau's miniature business card.

Tiny Tunes: In the 1930s, Robert L. Ratte played his 5.5-inch mini-violin on Robert Ripley's radio show.

Robo Gallery

Robots do all kinds of things these days, from playing soccer to aiding in search-and-rescue efforts to serving as pets!

Rescue Robots:

Fitted with video and infrared cameras, powerful lights and voice-activated microphones, these shoe-box-sized robots can crawl into tight spaces that are too small for humans or dogs. They were first used in New York to search for survivors after the collapse of the World Trade Center towers.

Robot League:

An annual robot soccer tournament attracts over 100 teams of mechanical players. The ultimate goal is to create a squad of robots that can take on and beat the best human players.

Slugfest:

A slug-hunting robot is being developed at the University of the West of England. When completed, it will be capable of catching 100 slugs an hour, which will later be used to generate electricity.

All the Buzz:

B.I.O.-Bugs from the Hasbro toy company are able to interact with their environment and change their behavior accordingly. Luckily, they can't sting!

Uncanny Canine:

The Sony AIBO robot dog (below) can recognize 75 words, respond to its name, see with infrared sensors, hear with the microphones in its ears, and move around like a real dog. It "learns" from interacting with its owner.

Purr-fectly Charming:

NeCoRo, a robot cat made by the Japanese manufacturer Omron, purrs when stroked, and gives other affectionate responses.

Kids' Stuff

Adults aren't the only ones who have cool ideas. Here are some of the clever inventions thought up by kids.

For the Birds: At the ages of 13 and 10, Esther and Annemarie Hoffman felt sorry for the birds because the squirrels always beat them to the feeder and gobbled up all the food. So the sisters invented a squirrel-proof bird feeder that worked so well, they formed their own company to market them.

Going Batty: Nine-year-old Austin Meggitt wanted to safely carry his bat and glove with him as he zipped around town on his bike. His invention, the Glove and Battie Caddie, later won him the Grand Prize in the Ultimate Invention Contest sponsored by the Discovery Channel.

Not So Fishy: When nine-year-old Eric Bunnelle's mother said he couldn't have a goldfish unless he figured out how to feed it while he was on vacation, he combined a telephone, a blinking light, and an electric massager to make his very own remote control fish feeder.

Cool Idea: In 1905, 11-year-old Frank Epperson stirred soda pop mix into a jar of water and left it out on the porch. The next morning, it was frozen around the stirring stick. In the summer, he made "Epsicles" in the icebox and started selling them. And this tasty treat is still being sold—only now it's called a Popsicle.

Bitter Sweet: After picking up the spiky "gum balls" dropped by the 16 sweet gum trees in her East Texas yard, 11-year-old Lindsey E. Clement decided to make the job easier. She invented the Gumball Machine to pick them up for her—and later won first place in the Craftsman/NSTA Young Inventor competition.

Just Plain Goofy

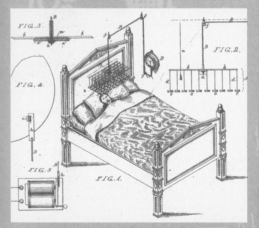

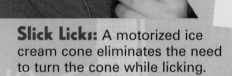

Slick Licks: A motorized ice cream cone eliminates the need to turn the cone while licking.

Fido Fooler: The aim of this toy-dog-and-vacuum-cleaner combo is to trick your pooch into thinking the vacuum cleaner is its friend.

Target Practice: In the middle of the night, toilet seat lights are just what's needed to keep things nice and tidy.

Rude Awakening: A lightweight frame suspended by ropes over a bed is guaranteed to wake even the heaviest of sleepers as soon as it falls down on his or her face.

Sounding It Out:

A robot guide for blind people designed in Japan emits ultrasound waves that bounce off obstacles. Then it will lead a blind person around them or, if it is not safe to proceed, wait until the obstacles disappear. It can even

plot the best route from start to finish. Unfortunately, it doesn't wag its tail or give its owner affection.

Toying with Baby:

California's Crump Institute for Medical Engineering has developed a breathing teddy bear that helps regulate a baby's sleep patterns while it monitors vital signs.

Chair-side Manner:

In the 1970s, therapists used the Alpha Chamber, a soft-cushioned, egg-shaped armchair with speakers, to help their patients through hypnosis, biofeedback, and relaxation training.

Stink-Free Shoes:

To combat smelly-feet syndrome, many companies are developing new lines of shoes, boots, and sandals that have been coated with AgION's silver-based antimicrobial compound. The fewer microbes floating around, the better your shoes are likely to smell.

All Hung Up: In 1903, when Albert J. Parkhouse arrived at his job at the Timberlake Wire and Novelty Company in Jackson, Michigan, there were no open coat hooks left. Without much thought, he reached for a piece of wire, bent it into two oblong hoops, twisted the ends together, and formed a hook in the middle. Then he hung his coat on it and went to work. The owners of the company liked the idea so much that they took out a patent on Parkhouse's idea. The company made a fortune, but Parkhouse, the inventor of the wire coat hanger, made nothing.

Wheeling and Dealing: In 1937, while watching his customers lug their groceries in handheld baskets up and down the aisles of his grocery store in Oklahoma City, Sylvan Goldman had what he thought was a brilliant idea: He invented the wheeled shopping cart and placed several in his store. But old habits die hard, and no one wanted to use them. It wasn't until he hired people to pretend they were shoppers and push the carts around the store that his idea finally started to catch on.

Imagine That!

Rows of buttons were first placed on shirtsleeves to . . .

a. prevent them from riding up beneath jacket sleeves.
b. keep people from wiping their noses on them.
c. help children learn how to count.
d. serve as decorations.

No Pressing Problems: Corpo Nove, a fashion company in Florence, Italy, has developed a fabric that needs no ironing. The Oricalco shirt is made of titanium-alloy fibers interwoven with nylon. No matter how wrinkled it gets, a few shots of air from a hair dryer will make the shirt look as if it came straight from the cleaners. The price tag? Four thousand dollars.

Avoiding Cat-astrophe: Englishman Percy Shaw was driving home one extremely dark and foggy night when he suddenly caught sight of a cat's eyes glowing in the dark. He stopped his car to avoid hitting the cat and realized that the cat had been sitting on a fence. Beyond the fence was a steep drop. If Shaw had not seen the cat first, he would have plunged over the cliff. That's when he got the idea for road reflectors—an idea that has since saved countless lives.

Imagine That!

Abul-Hassan, who in the 13th century, invented the hour by dividing the day into 24 equal parts, was . . .

a. an Indian novelist.
b. an Arabian poet.
c. an Egyptian engineer.
d. a Turkish mathematician.

 **Brain Buster**

What will they think of next? The following creations took a ton of imagination. But can you spot the one that is totally imaginary?

a. Just think! No more noisy, hard-to-start gas-powered lawn mowers. With Deanna Porath's combination tricycle and lawnmower, you can pedal around the yard, cutting the grass—while exercising at the same time.
Believe It!   **Not!**

b. Now you can hang art on your wall that will warm up the room at the same time. Gord Hamilton of Ontario, Canada, creates paintings that are embedded with hidden electric elements that act as heaters.
Believe It!   **Not!**

c. Jake & Jake Inc., a brother-in-law team from Maryland, crafted a must-have for the truly pampered pet. Their dog beds massage dogs' muscles, lulling tired pooches to sleep.
Believe It!   **Not!**

d. Checkers isn't just for two! A three-person checkerboard and a four-handed checkerboard were invented by Marion Hodges and Howard Wood respectively.
Believe It!   **Not!**

BONUS GAME

The following famous people made history. But can you match them up with their lesser-known creations?

1. Thomas Edison
2. Benjamin Franklin
3. Leonardo da Vinci
4. Thomas Jefferson
5. Sir Isaac Newton

a. A walking stick that converts into a stool
b. The harmonica
c. The wheelbarrow
d. Pet doors
e. Christmas tree lights

CHAPTER 5 Kids Incorporated

Here are some kid inventors who didn't give up until they found new ways to solve some old problems.

Imagine That!
When he was 11 years old, Antoine Vial of France invented a clothespin that alerted people that their laundry was dry by . . .

a. sounding a buzzer.
b. flashing a light.
c. turning blue.
d. dimming the house lights.

Wrist Warmers:
When the gap between 10-year-old Kathryn "K-K" Gregory's coat and mittens left her wrists cold and wet, she thought up Wristies. Not only have Wristies been a hit with kids but also with adults who work with their hands outside or in cold buildings, or who have arthritis, carpel tunnel syndrome, or circulation problems. K-K's invention has won her several awards as well as an appearance on *The Oprah Winfrey Show*.

Cool Idea: One winter night in 1905, 11-year-old Frank Epperson stirred powdered soda pop mix into a jar of water and left it out on the porch of his San Francisco home. That night the temperature dropped, hitting a record low. When Frank went outside the next morning, he found that the mixture had frozen around the stirring stick. The next summer, he made "Epsicles" in the icebox and started selling them. This tasty treat is still being sold—only now it's called a Popsicle.

Clean Sweep: Twelve-year-old Jennifer Garcia's job was to vacuum and sweep the dirt that was constantly being tracked into her home. "Why not vacuum dirty shoes instead?" she wondered. That's when she got the idea for the Vacuum Dirt Mat—which won the New York State competition of the Invent America! contest. When people see her invention, they always say, "Why didn't I think of that?" To which Jennifer replies, "Sometimes the best inventions are right in front of us, staring us in the face. We just have to keep looking for them."

Big Deal: In 1988, when she was 11 years old, Hannah Cannon of Hollywood, California, invented Cardz, a game that combined traditional playing cards with Scrabble. People in the toy business were so impressed with Hannah's game that she became the first child ever permitted on the floor of the International Toy Fair, the major annual toy-makers' convention.

Stub-Born: Some of Robbie Marcucci's favorite color crayons were too short to use. They would have gone to waste if he hadn't thought up the Crayon-Saver—an invention that works the same way a push-up pop does. Robbie's Crayon-Saver was such a hit that it won him the blue ribbon at his school's invention fair.

Imagine That!

At the age of four, John Parker of Vermont invented "ice star," a device that keeps . . .

a. ice cubes from sliding out of the glass while you're drinking.

b. shoes from slipping on ice.

c. ice-cream cones from dripping on your hands.

d. the blades of ice skates from getting dull.

On a Roll: Meredith Tucker loves to ice-skate and to in-line skate, too. So in 1997, at the age of 12, she invented Ice Blades, which utilizes a set of clip-on wheels to combine both skates in one. Now she doesn't have to waste time changing her skates when she zips home from the ice-skating rink in Shaker Heights, Ohio.

Noise Flash:
When he was eight years old, Brian Berlinski of Clifton, New Jersey, invented a silent car horn for the hearing-impaired—a light on the dashboard flashes at the sound of a honking horn.

Imagine That!

When they were eight and six years old, Sarah Cole Racine and her brother Brett invented edible tape to . . .

a. decorate food to make it more appetizing.
b. label food contents for finicky eaters.
c. personalize food portions so that everyone got an equal share.
d. make sloppy food easier to eat.

Handy Dipe and Wipe: When her baby brother needed changing, five-year-old Chelsea Lanmon of Texas fetched the powder, wipes, and diapers for her mother. If everything was packaged together, Chelsea figured she could save some time. So she sprinkled powder in a baby wipe, then folded it, and with her mother's help, sewed it up, and poked holes in it so that the powder would come out a little at a time. Next she made a pocket from the outside covering of one diaper and attached it to another one with double-edged tape. Chelsea won the national Invent America! competition for her invention, which she patented in 1994 at the age of eight.

Going Batty: In 1997, nine-year-old Austin Meggitt wanted to safely carry his bat and glove with him as he zipped around Amherst, Ohio, on his bike. His invention, the Glove and Battie Caddie, later won the Grand Prize in the Ultimate Invention contest sponsored by the Discovery Channel. In  1999, Austin was inducted into the National Gallery for America's Young Inventors at the National Inventors Hall of Fame.

Spotting Spot:

When he was six years old, Collin Hazen of North Dakota wanted a way to play ball with his dog on warm summer nights. The only trouble was that on a moonless night, it was hard to see

where the dog was. That's why Collin invented a battery-powered dog collar that glows in the dark.

Purr-fectly Edible: Six-year-old

Susan Goodin of Oklahoma loved her cats but hated washing the smelly food off the spoon when she fed them. When she heard about an invention contest, Susan had an idea. With some help from her grandmother, she came up with the Edible Cat Spoon, a garlic-flavored spoon that was strong enough to scoop the cat food from the can—and chewable as well. Now Susan just dumps the spoon in the bowl and her kitties get an extra treat. The cats are happy and so is Susan, who took first prize in the contest.

Imagine That!

In 1992, six-year-old James Jemtrud invented the Sucker Tucker for the purpose of . . .

a. keeping a baby's pacifier handy.
b. saving a straw to use again.
c. saving lollipops.
d. keeping a baby's bottle free of lint.

License to Win:

One day, ten-year-old Meghan Renee Hatfield was waiting with her mom in the checkout line at Kmart while the cashier copied her mother's license number onto the check. Meghan wondered why the cashier couldn't just stick the check in a slot and scan the license number into the cash register. Holding that thought, Meghan, who had twice entered the Invent America! contest but never won, decided to invent the Driver's License Number Scanner. As it turned out, three times was the charm. Meghan was the third-grade winner for the state of West Virginia.

No Fuss, No Muss:

A finalist in the 2001 Hammacher Schlemmer's Search for Invention competition, Carmina O'Connor of Illinois, has patented her Mashed Potato Machine, which cooks, mashes, and flavors potatoes in only 20 minutes. Just insert the potatoes, then add water and seasonings. The machine does the rest.

Dial-a-Meal:

What do you get when you combine a telephone, a phone flasher, an electric massager, and some fish food? A remote-control fish-feeder, of course. This invention was developed in the 1990s by nine-year-old Eric Bunnelle of Columbia, Missouri.

What inspired him? His mother said he could only have a goldfish if he could figure out how to feed it while he was on vacation.

Going Squirrelly:

When Esther and Annemarie Hoffman of Euclid, Ohio, were ages 13 and 10, they invented a bird-feeder made of recycled plastic bottles that's totally squirrel-proof.

Their first one was so successful that they've created a new and better model called The Transformer Bird Feeder. To market them, the girls (with a little help from their father) formed their own company, called Two Sisters and Their Dad.

Foul Ball!

Every fall, 11-year-old Lindsey Clement's Texas backyard is filled with spiky egg-shaped seedpods from 16 sweet gum trees. Besides being painful if stepped on, the seedpods are a pain to clean up. Lindsey decided to do something about it. She invented the Gumball Machine, which automatically picks up the seedpods and deposits them in a disposable bag. In 2000, her invention won her the Craftsman/NSTA Young Inventor Competition.

Imagine That!

When she was 11 years old, Melanie LaMontagne of Ontario, Canada, invented . . .

a. earmuffs for cats.
b. umbrellas for bird-feeders.
c. galoshes for guinea pigs.
d. snowshoes for dogs.

Tasty Fit: In 1992, when she was 11 years old, Elizabeth Anne Druback of New York invented a way to make visits to the dentist a little more enjoyable. She designed dental gloves called Flavor Fingers that come in root beer, coconut, and strawberry.

71

Imagine That!

Which of the following products was not invented by a kid?

a. LEGO toys
b. Magic Car Shine Wax
c. E. Z. Tools
d. The Tooth Fairy Light

Long Reach:

Jeanie Low of Texas invented a foldaway Kiddie Stool when she was still in kindergarten. One day, Jeanie's step stool fell apart because people kept stumbling over it. Since she needed a stool to reach the bathroom sink, her mom took her shopping for a new one. When Jeanie couldn't find what she had in mind—a stool that would always be there but could also be kept out of the way—she decided to invent one. The stool she designed and built with her father's help attaches to the cabinet door under the sink and has hinges that allow it to fold. Jeanie patented the design in 1992, and now others can buy her Kiddie Stools either ready-made or in a kit to put together themselves.

Kids say the darndest things . . . *and* they make cool inventions! The items below are all about clever kids and their crazy creations. Are you clever enough to catch the one that's been created just for you?

a. A kindergartner got off on the right foot when she was inspired to create a gadget called the "Surefooter." The device helps kids make sure they have their shoes on the right feet.

Believe It!   **Not!**

b. Nine-year-old Jennifer "Spitster" Roy of Hicksville, New York, was bored with the usual distance-based watermelon seed-spitting contests. So she started a new game by crafting a device to measure the speed at which the seeds were spit.

Believe It!   **Not!**

c. In 1955, Ronald Rolfe and Edward Manchester (both 15) combined parts from an old buggy and some farm machinery to create a real working automobile.

Believe It!   **Not!**

d. At the age of ten, Becky Shroder of Toledo, Ohio, invented a luminescent way of writing in the dark.

Believe It!   **Not!**

BONUS GAME

These five crafty kids came up with some pretty cool ideas. Can you match each creation to the age of its inventor?

1. A water-conserving sprinkler system by Larry Villella

2. Earmuffs by Chester Greenwood

3. Dissolving golf tees by Casey Golden

4. Insect-repelling laundry detergent by Brittany Cormier

5. Glow-in-the-dark toilet seats by Clint Lenz

a. 13
b. 15
c. 12
d. 6
e. 10

POP QUIZ

One more round! You know all about the *Incredible Inventions* in this book, right? Maybe you're thinking, *I could've created some of them myself.* Well then, strut your stuff by acing this pop quiz. (With five points for every correct answer, it will really boost your score, too!)

1. Which of the following *explosive* stories is true?

a. Pharmacist John Walker discovered matches when a flammable glob of chemicals stuck to his stirring stick.

b. The idea for firecrackers came about when a woman in 12th-century Malaysia accidentally ignited a barrel of gunpowder.

c. Jonathan Reiss, an engineer who grew up alongside an inactive volcano, invented a volcanic eruption detector when he was 13.

d. "Eternal Flame Candles" were invented and sold by Elvis fan Roslyn Gottlieb following the King's death in 1977. Some of the candles are still burning today.

2. Rubber is made from . . .

a. sand.

b. gum.

c. tree sap.

d. tree bark.

3. Three of the following toy stories are true. Can you tell which one is just playing with your mind?

a. The Slinky was invented by accident when Richard James tried to create a special spring for ship instruments.

b. Before getting its name, Silly Putty was used by circus clowns to make round red noses. It wasn't until 1943 that it was marketed as a toy.

c. Teddy bears were named for President Teddy Roosevelt after a particularly peaceful hunting trip.

d. Play-Doh was created by a man who was trying to come up with a new cleaning product.

4. Exploding golf balls that can be easily located were patented in 1990.

> **Believe It!**   **Not!**

5. Which of the following mechanical animals has *not* been invented, according to the files of Robert Ripley?

a. Cat

b. Bird

c. Dog

d. Monkey

6. Phrenology is the study of . . .

a. animal fears.

b. sleeping habits.

c. interpersonal relationships.

d. the shape of people's skulls.

7. Which of the following did Thomas Edison *not* invent?

a. The cement house

b. A perpetual cigar

c. A voice-powered sewing machine

d. The radio

8. In 1896, a 17-foot long tricycle was built to hold 15 people.

Believe It!   **Not!**

9. World's weirdest water vehicles! Which one of these is *not* to be believed? (Because it's not real!)

a. Water-wave in-line skates

b. A floating tricycle

c. An underwater bicycle

d. A PowerSki Jetboard

10. "The Real McCoy" refers to the famous inventor . . .

a. Lynn McCoy.

b. Abraham McCoy.

c. Elijah McCoy.

d. June McCoy.

11. Which one of the following innovations is nothing but "pure invention"?

a. A boat driven by wasps

b. Self-cleaning glass

c. Cow pagers

d. A baseball that displays its speed

12. Samuel Morse was inspired to invent the telegraph because . . .

a. he wanted to keep in touch with cousins who lived 200 miles away.

b. he worked on a ship that spent weeks at sea.

c. he was out of town when his wife died, and it took a week for the news to reach him.

d. war plans could be more easily communicated.

13. Which of the following will the Mini Autonomous Robot Vehicle Jr. (MARV Jr.) *not* be capable of doing?

a. Working in teams

b. Communicating with humans

c. Crawling through pipes

d. Navigating the ocean floor

14. An eight-year-old boy invented a silent car horn for the hearing-impaired.
Believe It!   Not!

15. Which of the following creative creations was *not* a kid's brainchild?

a. Edible tape

b. Ice-cream sundaes

c. Popsicles

d. Glow-in-the-dark dog collars

Answer Key

Chapter 1

Imagine That!

Page 5:   **b.** death.

Page 7:   **b.** sheer stupidity.

Page 8:   **a.** causing molecules in food to rub against each other.

Page 11:   **d.** vanilla.

Page 13:   **c.** Orthodontists use it to create dental molds.

Page 14:   **b.** three billion pounds of potatoes.

Page 16:   **d.** Life Savers

Page 18:   **b.** soap.

Brain Buster: d. is false.

Bonus Game: 1=c; 2=d; 3=a; 4=b; 5=e

Chapter 2

Imagine That!

Page 21:   **d.** lit a candle.

Page 23:   **a.** mouse ears.

Page 25:   **b.** snoring.

Page 27:   **d.** last breath.

Page 29:   **a.** a needle.

Page 30:   **b.** famous people.

Page 32:   **d.** jalapeño peppers.

Page 34:   **d.** deicer on highways.

Brain Buster: c. is false.

Bonus Game: 1=a; 2=b; 3=e; 4=c; 5=d

Chapter 3

Imagine That!

Page 37:   **c.** a model of a horse's head in front.

Page 39:   **c.** filter car fumes.

Page 40:   **d.** Abraham Lincoln.

Page 43:   **c.** porcelainized bathtub.

Page 44:   **b.** an ever-saddled horse that eats nothing.

Page 46:   **a.** ammonia.

Brain Buster: **a.** is false.

Bonus Game: 1=d; 2=c; 3=e; 4=a; 5=b

Chapter 4

Imagine That!

Page 49:   **b.** George Washington Carver

Page 51:   **c.** wife's wedding dress.

Page 52:   **c.** the washing machine.

Page 55:   **a.** sermons.

Page 56:   **a.** the weapon that caused it.

Page 59:   **b.** keep people from wiping their noses on them.

Page 60:   **b.** an Arabian poet.

Brain Buster: **c.** is false.

Bonus Game: 1=e; 2=b; 3=c; 4=a; 5=d

Chapter 5

Imagine That!

Page 63: **b.** flashing a light.

Page 65: **a.** ice cubes from sliding out of the glass while you're drinking.

Page 66: **d.** make sloppy food easier to eat.

Page 68: **c.** saving lollipops.

Page 71: **d.** snowshoes for dogs.

Page 72: **a.** LEGO toys

Brain Buster: b. is false.

Bonus Game: 1=c; 2=b; 3=a; 4=d; 5=e

Pop Quiz

1. **a.**
2. **c.**
3. **b.**
4. **Believe It!**
5. **b.**
6. **d.**
7. **d.**
8. **Not!**
9. **a.**
10. **c.**
11. **a.**
12. **c.**
13. **d.**
14. **Believe It!**
15. **b.**

What's Your Ripley's Rank?

Ripley's Scorecard

Well done! You've busted those brain cells over some of the world's most wacky gadgets and gizmos. Now it's time to tally up your answers and get your Ripley's rating. Are you just **Making a Start**? Or were you **Meant to Invent**? Add up your scores to find out!

Here's the scoring breakdown—give yourself:

★ **10 points** for every **Imagine That!** you answered correctly;

★ **20 points** for every fiction you spotted in the **Ripley's Brain Busters**;

★ **2** for every match you made on the **Bonus Games**;

★ and **5** for every **Pop Quiz** question you answered correctly.

Here's a tally sheet:

Number of **Imagine That**
questions answered correctly: _____ x 10 = _____
Number of **Ripley's Brain Buster**
fictions spotted: _____ x 20 = _____
Number of **Bonus Games**
matches made: _____ x 2 = _____
Number of **Pop Quiz** questions
answered correctly: _____ x 5 = _____

Total the right column for your final score: _____

0-100
Making a Start

Okay, so you're not exactly bursting with the creative power of invention. But you made it this far! And the amazing world of Ripley's is sucking you in . . . slowly. With some patience, you'll no doubt develop that weird and wacky Ripley's insight into separating fact from fiction. And once that starts, inventive behavior may be just around the corner!

101-250
Discovering Daily

The creative juices are flowing! You're really starting to get into all these extraordinary innovations. But you need to embrace your inner Ripley by brushing up on all of his bizarre factoids. Knowledge is power, my friend, and with a little more insight into the unusual, you'll be on your way to becoming a real Ripley's-style inventor.

251-400
Constantly Creating

Gadgets, gizmos, and wacky stuff is all you. You've certainly got the 411 on unbelievable inventions and discoveries—and you're not afraid to flaunt it. Separating fact from fiction like a pro, you almost reach the level of Robert Ripley himself. But of course, there's always more discovering to be done . . . .

401-575
Meant to Invent

Congratulations! You've reached the blissful state of Ripley's genius. In fact, maybe you know a little *too* much. All that bizarre info taking up space in your head—it may not be so healthy! You're both a gadget guru *and* a Ripley's groupie. Know what that means? It's time for you to invent something totally wacky yourself so that *you* can go down in Ripley's history.

Believe It!®

Photo Credits

Ripley Entertainment Inc. and the editors of this book wish to thank the following photographers, agents, and other individuals for permission to use and reprint the following photographs in this book. Any photographs included in this book that are not acknowledged below are property of the Ripley Archives. Great effort has been made to obtain permission from the owners of all materials included in this book. Any errors that may have been made are unintentional and will gladly be corrected in future printings if notice is sent to Ripley Entertainment Inc., 5728 Major Boulevard, Orlando, Florida 32819.

Black & White Photos

5 X-ray/Worldwide rights, excluding countries that do not recognize U.S. copyright protection, courtesy of the American College of Radiology

6 Arthur Fry; 10 Patsy Sherman/3M

6 Safety Pins; 3, 25 Dimple-making Machine/ U.S. Patent and Trademark Office

12 Theodore Roosevelt Cartoon/Copyright Unknown

15 Ice-cream Sundaes; 17 Chocolate-chip Cookies/CORBIS

27 Thomas Edison/National Park Service/Edison National Historic Site

28 One-hand Clock/R. O. Schmitt Fine Arts

31 Max Factor/Proctor & Gamble Cosmetics/Noxell Corporation

34 Nikola Tesla/Tesla Wardenclyffe Project Archives

37 AUTOnomy Concept Car/2002 General Motors Corporation. Used with permission of GM Media Archives

38 Lunar Roving Vehicle/NASA

40 Edmund Halley/Royal Astronomical Society Library

41 PowerSki Jetboard/PowerSki International Corporation

42 SoloTrek™ XFV®/MJI

42 M400 Skycar/Moller International

45 Steve Roberts on BEHEMOTH/Nomadic Research Labs/www.microship.com

46 Rollerman/Christophe Lebedinsky

51 Samuel Morse/Evert A. Duyckinick Portrait Gallery of Eminent Men and Women in Europe and America. New York: Johnson, Wilson & Company, 1873

54 MARV Jr./Sandia National Laboratories

56 Remote-Control Surgery/Computer Motion, Inc.

58 Albert J. Parkhouse/Gary Mussell

63 Kathryn "K-K" Gregory wearing Wristies®/H. Scott Gregory, Jr.

67 Austin Meggitt/Anne Meggit

69 Mashed Potato Machine/Hammacher Schlemmer

70 Esther and Annemarie Hoffman/Dennis Hoffman/Two Sisters and Their Dad

71 Lindsey Clement/Craftsman/NSTA

Color Insert

Ian Ashpole/Flying Pictures

Tricycle Catamaran/courtesy Raymond Little

Icy Rider/Bo Nordell

Search-and-Rescue Robots/JPL/NASA

Robot Soccer/James Bruce, Carnegie Mellon University

Slugbot/Intelligent Autonomous Systems Laboratory, University of the West of England

B.I.O.-Bugs/Hasbro and Litzky Public Relations

NeCoRo/OMROM Corporation

Sony AIBO Robot Dog/Sony Electronics Inc./Entertainment Robot America

Esther and Annmarie Hoffman/Dennis Hoffman/Two Sisters and Their Dad

Austin Meggitt/Anne Meggitt

Eric Bunnelle/Eric Bunnelle

Lindsey Clement/Craftsman/NSTA

Frank Epperson; Popsicle/Good Humor-Breyers Ice Cream

Motorized Ice-Cream Cone/Rick Hartman/ The Toymaker's Workshop/ www.toyworkshop.com

Toy-Dog-and-Vacuum Cleaner; Rude Awakening/U.S. Patent and Trademark Office

Toilet Seat Lights/Laura Miller

Cover

SoloTrek™ XFV®/MJI

Robot Soccer/James Bruce, Carnegie Mellon University

Tricycle Catamaran/courtesy Raymond Little

Don't miss these other exciting

books . . .

World's Weirdest Critters

Creepy Stuff

Odd-inary People

Amazing Escapes

Bizarre Bugs

If you enjoyed **World's Weirdest Gadgets**, get ready for

 **Blasts from the Past**

It may be hard to believe, but everything you're about to read is true!

George Washington was not the first president of the United States

During the French Revolution, soldiers were armed with umbrella guns to protect them from the sun and rain

During the flagpole-sitting craze that started in the late 1920s, a man called "Shipwreck" Kelly was the best—once sitting on a flagpole for 49 days straight

Famous chef Julia Child was a spy during World War II

It's time to set the record straight and to fill in the gaps with some of the most entertaining but little-known facts in history. Read all about them in **Blasts from the Past.**